Meet Dave.

He's always been different
than the other kids.
He's tall, taller than the other
kids in his class.
He's skinny,
skinnier than the
other kids in his class.
He's so tall and skinny that he
gets teased, a lot.
His pants aren't long enough
and he's got
patches on his knees
and his shoes are old.
His hair looks funny
because of something
called a cowlick,
one in the back
and one in the front.

Kids make fun of him in class

and at recess and in gym and at lunch and on the bus.

They call him names like

"Twiggy" and "Melvin" and

"Stickman" and "Freak."

Sometimes he feels sad and alone.

He feels strange

and weird

and unusual

and different.

(Do you ever feel different?)

So, he wishes they

didn't notice him.

He wishes he could blend in.

He wishes he was normal.

Adults don't seem to like him very much either.

He gets in trouble, a lot.

His teachers tell him

to sit still and

be quiet

and stop goofing around

and do what

they tell him to do.

6

He tries.

But, he can't seem to sit still or be

quiet or stop goofing around or do

what they tell him to do.

They call him immature

and **obnoxious** and **inappropriate** and **immature** and **rebellious** and **undisciplined**.

Those are big words and he doesn't even know what they mean,

but he's pretty sure they're not good.

He thinks they're bad words and that he's bad too.

Sometimes the teachers get so

mad that they send him to see

the principal.

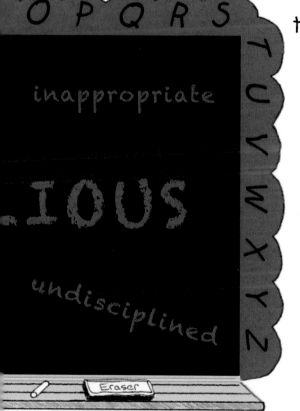

The principal says he's out of control

and needs to pay attention

and needs more self discipline

and needs to

grow up.

His parents

agree with the

teacher and the

principal,

so they send him

to the school

counselor.

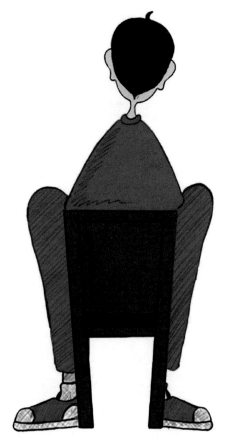

The counselor uses words like

oppositional and **defiant** and **deficit** and **hyperactive** and **disorder** and **medication**.

Those are big words and he doesn't even know what they mean, but he's pretty sure they're not good. He thinks they're bad words and that he's bad too.

Everyone thinks something is wrong with Dave

and sometimes he agrees with them.

(Do you ever feel like something is wrong with you?)

He wishes he could be normal and ordinary.

He wishes he could fit in.

He wishes that he didn't stick out.

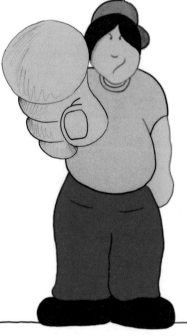

He wishes he wasn't different.

He wishes he was shorter and not so

skinny and quieter and not so hyper.

He wishes he could be good like the

other kids and like his parents and

teachers want him to be.

So, he spends his life trying to be

normal in junior high and high school

and college and at work.

But, it didn't work.

And then one day, everything changed.

He started to see

that everything

that made him **different**

was **good**, not bad.

He found out

it was good

to be a freak.

15

He was tall

and that made him

good at basketball.

The other kids weren't laughing

when he got a scholarship

to college.

They wished they
could be tall like him.

He was skinny and hyperactive

and couldn't
sit still

and that made him

good at running.

The other kids weren't

laughing when he ran his

first marathon.

They wished they could
be skinny and fit and
full of energy like him.

He talked too much

and that made him a good speaker.

The other kids weren't laughing when

he started making presentations

all over the world.

They wished they could be articulate like him.

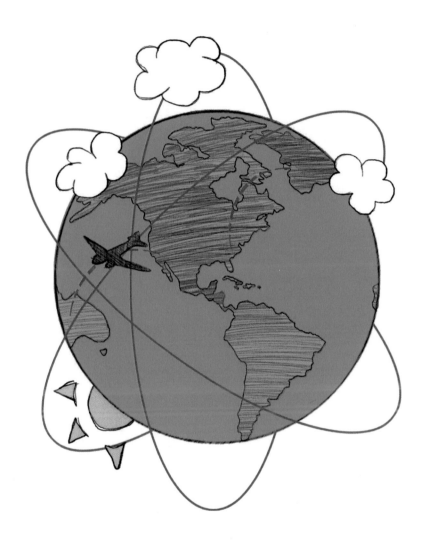

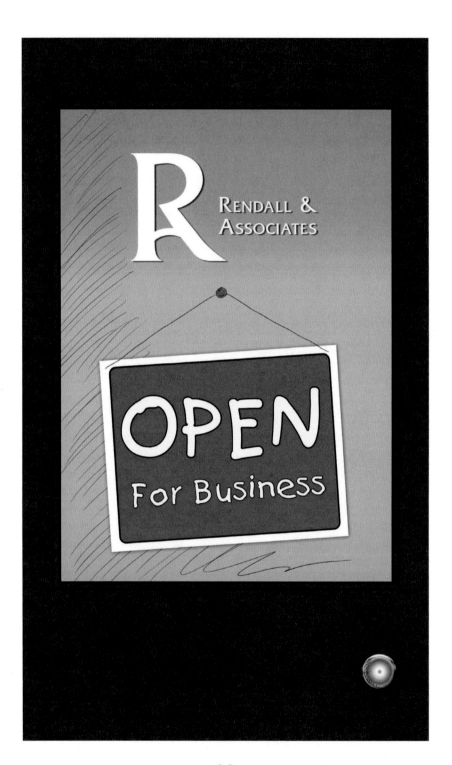

He couldn't do what he was told

and that made him a

good entrepreneur.

The other kids weren't laughing when

he started his own business.

They wished they could be courageous like him.

He was silly and immature and goofed around a lot

and that made him **very funny.**

The other kids weren't laughing when

he did stand up comedy.

(Well, they were laughing, but you

know what I mean.)

They wished they could be humorous like him.

The other kids

(well, they were all grown up now)

wished they were **different**
and **weird** and **strange** and
unusual because that would make
them **interesting** and **original**
and **special** and **distinctive**.

25

They
wished
they were
freaks
and
so did
he.

He wanted to help them become freaks like him.

For the first time he was proud that he was different and proud to be a freak. He didn't want to be normal anymore.

He wanted to be **more weird** and **more strange** and **more different** and **more unusual** and to help other people to be freaks just like him.

Sometimes things turn out better than they start.

Sometimes the weirdest kids make the best adults.

Parenting

A number of years ago my friend's wife, Lynn, asked me to do a parenting presentation for a women's group. I was happy to do the talk, but a little apprehensive. Because the meeting was just for women, I would be the only man in the room.

To make matters worse, at the time of the presentation, I didn't have any children. My only qualifications were academic, since I had undergraduate and graduate degrees in counseling psychology. This probably wouldn't count for much since I already had two major strikes against me. I was a man with no children who telling mothers and grandmothers how to care for their offspring.

Fortunately, Lynn assured me that my failure to procreate would not be a problem. She had an introduction that would give me the credibility I needed to win over the audience. She started by listing my qualifications and then explained that I had been a friend of her husband's since high school. Apparently, he had shared many stories with her about my past and his revelations had led her to an important conclusion.

The final words of her introduction were, "The reason you should listen to Dave is because he is proof that even your really bad kids can turn out okay." Ouch! In other words, he has secret knowledge about the inner workings of difficult children. Maybe he has some special insights to share from his checkered past.

I want to focus on her final phrase. I'm a bad kid that turned out okay. How exactly did that happen? Was I really a bad kid? What lessons can we learn from that experience that will improve our parenting? As you know from reading the rest of the book, I turned out okay by applying the seven-part framework from The Freak Factor book. The first part is awareness.

Awareness

When it comes to parenting there are two levels of awareness. First is your ability to identify your child's strengths and weaknesses. Second is their understanding of their own strengths and weaknesses.

You can use the following assessment to improve your awareness of your child's unique characteristics and the connections between their weaknesses and strengths. However, I have also created an assessment for your child to do on their own or with your help. Additionally, I made a list of questions to help your child improve their self-awareness and think about how they can apply their distinctive qualities.

1. **What is something you are good at?**

   Something I am good at is _____

   _____

2. **What is something you do that other people don't like?**

   Something I do that others don't like is _____

   _____

3. **What is something that you wish you could change about yourself?**

   I wish I could change _____ about myself.

4. **How can you do the opposite of what everyone else is doing?**

   I can do the opposite of what everyone else is doing by _____

   _____

5. **How can you get even better at something you do well?**

   I can make something I am good at even better by _____

   _____

6. **How can you stick out instead of trying to fit in?**

   I can stick out instead of trying to fit in by_____

   _____

7. **Of everything you have done, what is the one thing you are the most proud of?**

   Of everything I have done, I am the most proud of _____

   _____

8. **What was the happiest day of your life? What were you doing?**

The happiest day of my life was when _____

_____

9. **What is your favorite subject in school? Which part do you like best?**

My favorite subject in school is _____

because _____

10. **What is your favorite job or chore? What do you like best about it?**

My favorite job or chore is _____

because _____

11. **What job or chore do you hate to do? What do you hate about it?**

The job or chore I hate to do is _____

What I hate most about it is _____

12. **What subject in school do you dislike? Which part do you hate the most about it?**
The subject in school I dislike is _____ because

13. **Which kind of activities do you put off doing until you have to?**

An activity I put off doing until I have to is _____

_____

14. **What activities make you tired?**

I get tired when I have to _____

_____

1. Put a check in the box next to your strengths (a strength is something that is good about you).

2. If you notice a trait that is definitely not one of your strengths, draw a line through it.

3. Choose your top three strengths.

X	Strength	X	Strength
	1. I am **creative** and have new ideas about how something can be done.		14. I am **independent** and do things without help from others.
	2. I am **organized**. When I do something, I am careful and pay attention to details.		15. I am a **team-player** and am more concerned for other people than I am for myself.
	3. I am **dedicated**. I try to do something even though it is difficult or other people want me to stop.		16. I am **sensitive**. I am caring.
	4. I am **flexible**. I can adapt in order to fit or work better in a situation.		17. I am **humble**. I do not think of myself as better than other people.
	5. I am **enthusiastic**. I express strong emotions.		18. I am **confident** and do not worry a lot.
	6. I am **calm**. I am relaxed.		19. I am **spontaneous**. I make decisions quickly.
	7. I have a lot of **energy**. I am very active.		20. I am a **leader**. I can influence other people.
	8. I am **thoughtful** and think carefully about things.		21. I am **relaxed**. I am easygoing.
	9. I am **adventurous**. I am very brave.		22. I am **serious**. I am mature.
	10. I am **responsible**. I am careful about avoiding danger and risk.		23. I am **funny**. I am amusing.
	11. I am **honest**. I do not waste time and get right to the point.		24. I am **generous**. I like to use what I have to help others.
	12. I am **polite**. I am respectful. I am courteous.		25. I am **curious**. I have a desire to know and learn more.
	13. I am **competitive** and determined to win.		

#1 Strength:_____   #2 Strength:_____   #3 Strength:_____

1. Put a check in the box next to your weaknesses (a weakness is something that is not good about you).

2. If you notice a trait that is definitely not one of your weaknesses, draw a line through it.

3. Choose your top three weaknesses.

X	Weakness	X	Weakness
	1. I am sloppy and **messy**. I am disorganized.		14. I am **selfish**. I only care about myself.
	2. I don't like to change.		15. I need a lot of help from others. I need a lot of attention.
	3. I am **stubborn**.		16. I am **easily hurt**. I am easily upset.
	4. I have a hard time keeping my promises.		17. I am **not confident** about myself or my abilities.
	5. I become **angry** quickly and easily.		18. I have too much pride in myself. I am **over-confident**.
	6. I am **not sympathetic** toward other people.		19. I am **impatient**. I don't like to wait. I do things without thinking.
	7. I **worry** a lot. I usually feel nervous.		20. I am **bossy**. I'm always telling people what to do.
	8. I am quiet. I am **shy**.		21. I am **lazy**.
	9. I **don't worry** about the consequences of my actions.		22. I am **too serious**. I am not very fun.
	10. I am **boring**. I am not very interesting.		23. I am **too silly**. I am immature.
	11. I am **rude**. I am not polite.		24. I am easily fooled. I am easily tricked.
	12. I don't always tell people how I really feel. I don't want to hurt their feelings.		25. I am **nosy**. I get too involved in other people's business.
	13. I care about winning more than anything else.		

#1 Weakness: _____   #2 Weakness: _____   #3 Weakness: _____

Acceptance

Parents have a powerful influence on their children. However, this influence can sometimes be quite negative. In *The Element,* Ken Robinson tells the story of Paulo Coelho, a young man who wanted to be a writer. Unfortunately, his parents thought that Paulo should be a lawyer and that writing was nothing more than a hobby. When Paulo resisted their advice and pursued his writing career, his parents had him committed to a psychiatric institution where he was given electroshock treatments.

His parents did this because they loved him and wanted what was best for him. But their notions of what was best included having a normal life with a good job doing respectable work that paid a good salary. The believed that their job as parents was to change Paulo from who he was, and who he wanted to be, into what they felt he should be. They weren't able to accept his uniqueness.

Matt Langdon at *The Hero Construction Company* teaches kids that they can be heroes in everyday situations. One of Matt's posts about the movie *The Tale of Despereaux* argues that it is good to be strange. The post begins with a quote from the movie, which is a cartoon about a mouse with extraordinarily large ears and tremendous courage.

"Reader, you must know that an interesting fate awaits almost everyone, mouse or man, who **does not conform.**' When you act heroically, you're going to **stand out**. Despereaux's ears were not the only thing that made people notice him. His courage, thoughts of a better world, and kindness made him stand out.

They also **made him the object of disdain and mockery.**
Heroes are ordinary people who do extraordinary things, so
there will always be a majority to think the hero's behavior is
wrong, dangerous, or weird. Heroes don't cower and they don't
subscribe to the ideas of the masses just because those ideas
are popular."

If we want our children to be extraordinary, we need to make sure
that we aren't implicitly or explicitly forcing them to conform to
narrow standards of normalcy.

Remember negativity bias? When your child brings home a report
card, what do you focus on? Do you talk about the good grades
or the bad grades? Do you try to build on their strengths or fix
their weaknesses?

Once I brought home a report card with an A in every subject,
except English. I was getting a C in that class. How did my parents respond? Did they compliment me on my excellent work in
most of my classes? Did they encourage me to focus my efforts
on those areas where I was having success? No. Instead, they
wanted to talk about English. What was I doing wrong? How
could I do better? Was I trying hard enough? They believed, as
most parents do, that we all need to be well-rounded.

The people who are closest to us are the most likely to uncover
and address our deepest flaws. We might be able to hide some
weaknesses from others but our families tend to know us better
than anyone else.

Acceptance begins by recognizing that our children's weaknesses are also strengths. It is about seeing the upside, instead of just the down-side. Let's continue the assessment and try to find the connections between your child's weaknesses and strengths.

1. Make a list of the top three strengths and weaknesses that you identified in the awareness section.

2. Put a check mark next to each of them on the chart below.

3. Are there any matches? (a match is when you selected a strength and a weakness in the same row).

Strengths | Weaknesses

	Strengths		Weaknesses	
1.	I am **creative** and have new ideas about how something can be done.	1.	I am sloppy and **messy**. I am disorganized.	
2.	I am **organized**. When I do something, I am careful and pay attention to details.	2.	I don't like to change.	
3.	I am **dedicated**. I try to do something even though it is difficult or other people want me to stop.	3.	I am **stubborn**.	
4.	I am **flexible**. I can adapt in order to fit or work better in a situation.	4.	I have a hard time keeping my promises.	
5.	I am **enthusiastic**. I express strong emotions.	5.	I become **angry** quickly and easily.	
6.	I am **calm**. I am relaxed.	6.	I am **not sympathetic** toward other people.	
7.	I have a lot of **energy**. I am very active.	7.	I **worry** a lot. I usually feel nervous.	
8.	I am **thoughtful** and think carefully about things.	8.	I am quiet. I am **shy**.	
9.	I am **adventurous**. I am very brave.	9.	I **don't worry** about the consequences of my actions.	
10.	I am **responsible**. I am careful about avoiding danger and risk.	10.	I am **boring**. I am not very interesting.	

Strengths	Weaknesses	
11. I am **honest**. I do not waste time and get right to the point.	11. I am **rude**. I am not polite.	
12. I am **polite**. I am respectful. I am courteous.	12. I don't always tell people how I really feel. I don't want to hurt their feelings.	
13. I am **competitive** and determined to win.	13. I care about winning more than anything else.	
14. I am **independent** and do things without help from others.	14. I am **selfish**. I only care about myself.	
15. I am a **team-player**. I'm more concerned for other people than I am for myself.	15. I need a lot of help from others. I need a lot of attention.	
16. I am **sensitive**. I am caring.	16. I am **easily hurt**. I am easily upset.	
17. I am **humble**. I do not think of myself as better than other people.	17. I am **not confident** about myself or my abilities.	
18. I am **confident** and do not worry a lot.	18. I have too much pride in myself. I am **over-confident**.	
19. I am **spontaneous**. I make decisions quickly.	19. I am **impatient**. I don't like to wait. I do things without thinking.	
20. I am a **leader**. I can influence other people.	20. I am **bossy**. I'm always telling people what to do.	
21. I am **relaxed**. I am easygoing.	21. I am **lazy**.	
22. I am **serious**. I am mature.	22. I am **too serious**. I am not very fun.	
23. I am **funny**. I am amusing.	23. I am **too silly**. I am immature.	
24. I am **generous**. I like to use what I have to help others.	24. I am easily fooled. I am easily tricked.	
25. I am **curious**. I have a desire to know and learn more.	25. I am **nosy**. I get too involved in other people's business.	

37

Appreciation

Appreciation isn't always easy. My youngest daughter, Sophia, was at her first day of kindergarten. At snack time, the teacher asked each child if they had something to eat and drink. Sophia told the teacher that she had a snack. We had packed some crackers and a small bottle of water.

But then something unexpected happened. A few of the kids didn't have a snack. They either forgot or their parents weren't aware that they needed one.

The teacher didn't want these kids to be left out, so she gave some cookies and juice to each of the kids who didn't have a snack. Sophia didn't like that at all. She had been responsible and brought her snack, but it was just plain crackers and water. Now these kids, who hadn't followed the rules, were getting rewarded with juice and cookies. She wanted juice and cookies, but she'd already told the teacher she had a snack. What could she do?

She raised her hand. When the teacher called on her, she said "I forgot. I'm allergic to water." This is funny but it is also disconcerting. This wasn't Sophia's first lie. She lies regularly, even about things that don't matter. It would be easy to start to see her as a bad person, as fundamentally dishonest. But there is another perspective.

Researchers have found a link between dishonesty and intellectual development in children. In other words, it takes a certain level of intelligence to tell a good lie and children can't lie until their brain has reached a particular stage of development. Additionally, people with higher IQs tend to lie more often.

There's something else you should know about Sophia. She is very imaginative. For example, she has innumerable dolls and stuffed animals and she can play with them for hours, making up elaborate stories about their pretend adventures.

This doesn't mean that I condone her dishonesty or tell her that it's acceptable to lie. I don't. However, I do see that there is an upside. I appreciate the strengths, imagination and intelligence, that correspond to this particular weakness, dishonesty. I haven't branded her as a bad child because I see there's another side to the story.

Sophia is also very stubborn. This can be very frustrating. When you tell her that she can't have something, she will continue asking you incessantly in the hopes that she will wear you down. As much as I don't like to admit this, there is an upside to this as well. She is very persistent.

My job as a parent is to acknowledge, appreciate and encourage her persistence because I know that it is a positive trait which will serve her very well as an adult. Again, it is my prerogative to tell her that I don't appreciate being nagged and to avoid giving in to her, but I shouldn't criticize her as stubborn and tell her that it is a bad trait she needs to eliminate. That isn't true and it's not helpful.

Amplification

If we truly appreciated our children's unique qualities, we would find ways to help them exaggerate those qualities. We would help them amplify, instead of moderating or minimizing their unusual characteristics.

Adam's parents remember that he was always screaming as a child. Adam explains, "Apparently, I was a real pain in the butt in restaurants. They couldn't take me anywhere. I was super super noisy. . . I was very talkative, very hyperactive. I was bouncing off the walls all the time. Not much different than I am now really." He was noisy, so they told him to be quiet. They even stopped taking him out because it was embarrassing to have a child who wasn't normal and quiet and obedient.

Adam has grown up but he's still screaming and noisy and now he has a full band and sound system to accompany him and amplify his voice. Although his parents used to tell him to be quiet, I bet they're happy that he didn't listen. Because he was the runner-up on *American Idol* in 2009 and his first album sold nearly a million copies worldwide, more than Kris Allen, the 2009 winner.

We shouldn't wait until someone else helps our child amplify their strengths and weaknesses. It's possible that no one ever will. We need to be the ones that encourage our children to be more of who they are.

Alignment

Last year, I was watching the classic TV version of *Rudolph the Red-Nosed Reindeer* and realized that it beautifully illustrates the importance of alignment, finding the right fit.

"Rudolph the red-nosed reindeer had a very shiny nose, and if you ever saw it, you would even say it glows."

Rudolph was different. He had a major and obvious flaw. He was a freak. This is the same for most of us. We are different. We have flaws. We are too impatient or too messy or too organized or too serious or too loud or too quiet. We are freaks.

"All of the other reindeer used to laugh and call him names. They never let poor Rudolph, join in any reindeer games."

Rudolph's flaw made him unpopular and led to his rejection and isolation. No one wants to be rejected. So what do we do? We often try to hide our flaws and fix our weaknesses. We become ashamed. We wish we could just be normal, like everyone else. We want to be accepted, so we try to change.

This is just what Rudolph and his parents tried to do. They covered up his nose with a black rubber cone, but it didn't work. The red nose still shone through. It looked like Rudolph was destined for a life of pain and misery, but then the situation changed.

"Then one foggy Christmas Eve, Santa came to say, Rudolph with your nose so bright, won't you guide my sleigh tonight?"

Rudolph's nose wasn't really a weakness. It was a strength in disguise. In the right situation, a "foggy Christmas Eve," Rudolph's nose was an irreplaceable advantage. When the situation changed, the value of his unique characteristic changed as well.

What made him a freak also made him a hero. He didn't succeed in spite of his weakness; he succeeded because of his weakness. What would have happened if Rudolph would have gone to Hollywood and gotten a nose job?

"Then all the reindeer loved him and they shouted out with glee, Rudolph the Red-Nosed Reindeer, you'll go down in history."

Rudolph's legacy, his enduring fame, was a result of a perfect fit between his unique qualities and the situation.

Do you want your children to succeed? Do you want them to make history or at least make a difference? Help them find their foggy Christmas Eve. Look to their apparent weaknesses and flaws. They are strengths in disguise. They offer clues to how they can make a unique contribution. Don't try to hide them or fix them. Just find the right situation, the one that offers the perfect fit between who they are and what is required. Unlike Rudolph, we don't have to just wait for the right situation to come along; we can seek it out or even create it.

Michael Phelps is the most successful Olympian of all time. He has more medals than anyone else. But he also has ADHD. So his mom had a decision to make. Should she give him medicine to "fix" his ADHD or should she help him find a situation that rewarded him for his hyperactivity? Athletics is a situation that rewards children for the same characteristics they are punished for at school. Michael's mom realized that she didn't need to change him, she needed to change the situation. If she couldn't change who he was, she could change where he was.

When it comes to kids, one of the problems with alignment is that school is one, very specific situation that lasts for their entire childhood. A failure to fit in at school can leave parents and children feeling like failures. But as we have seen many times in this book, how a person does in school isn't always a predictor of the level of success they will achieve in life. Furthermore, even though we spend most of our childhood in school, we spend most of our life outside of school.

Nevertheless, school success is a major concern for many parents. Here are a few suggestions.

Start by considering alternative schools (art, music, drama, dance, engineering, etc.). Montessori schools, online education, and home schooling are other options. Unconventional education can be a good fit for unconventional kids.

If this isn't an option, and it isn't for many parents, there are other things you can do. Look for extracurricular activities within the school that are a good match with your child's unique qualities. Sports, band, debate, choir, student government and many other activities help kids who don't fit in to find a place they fit. If you can't change the larger situation (school), try to find or create other situations that give your child a different, and more positive, perspective on their strengths and weaknesses.

If your child gets in trouble at school for misbehavior, the way you handle that at home has a big impact on your child. I got punished again at home for things I had already been punished for at school. The message was clear, if the teacher thinks you are bad, then you are bad.

We need to be careful when we give other adults this kind of power to decide what is good or bad about our child. Sometimes we need to contextualize the misbehavior. For example, the teacher says that the child is immature and has no self-control because they talk too much. You can support the teacher's right to manage the class in the way they see fit, but also let your child know that their behavior, although inappropriate in that situation, is also evidence of positive qualities that can be used at the right place and the right time.

The next thing to do is to create the right place and the right time for your child to be unique. I was always being told that this wasn't the time or place for me to be myself. But it seemed like the time never came and we never arrived at the place. If your child is hyper, get them more time in the yard and on the playground. Sign them up for local sports teams. If your child is creative, but messy, get them in an art class. Help them to discover where they fit. Give them outlets for their uniqueness.

Avoidance

My oldest daughter, Anna, isn't very athletic. She isn't very coordinated. She doesn't like groups and the chaos of team sports. She is independent. She doesn't like to get sweaty. She doesn't want to get hurt. She isn't competitive. When it was time to sign up for fall or spring sports at her school, we would ask her if she wanted to play. She always declined. One year, when we asked her about it she said, "sports just isn't my thing."

Although I was very athletic and I know the value of sports, I never forced her to join a team. I allowed her to avoid activities that weren't a good fit. This is the other side of alignment. We need to help our kids find the right fit and we also need to allow them to avoid activities that don't match their interests and abilities. It needs to be okay for them to say that something is "not their thing."

When she was in sixth grade, Anna signed up for the new swimming team. It was the perfect fit (alignment). She is tall and thin. Swimming is repetitive and doesn't require a lot of coordination. It is very safe. She isn't going to get hit with a ball or fall on the ground. She can be independent. Swimming requires a very low level of teamwork and cooperation. It's also hard to get sweaty in the pool.

This brings us to the subject of quitting. Sometimes kids don't realize that something isn't their thing until they've already started. As we've already discussed, I'm a big fan of quitting. I think it's great to encourage kids to try new things, how else will they know what they like and what they don't like. Experimenting is an important part of developing their self-awareness. However, they'll be less open to trying new things when we have an absolute "no quitting" policy. My youngest daughter has quit soccer, dance and gymnastics. She still hasn't found her thing, but she will.

Affiliation

Home is a great place to learn teamwork. It's a great place for kids to learn that they don't have to do everything and that different people can work together to accomplish mutual goals. Look for opportunities to use your children's complementary strengths. For example, maybe one of your kids is very organized and does a great job loading the dishwasher to maximum capacity. But another kid loves to be outside and enjoys yard work. We don't need to force each child to do an equal amount of the same work. We can allow them each to contribute by using their unique strengths.

The main idea is that childhood is a great time to learn about both interdependence and uniqueness. We can help our kids learn to contribute to a group objective by offering our best individual talents.

About the author

During the last fifteen years, David Rendall has spoken to audiences on every inhabited continent. His clients include the US Air Force, Australian Government, and Fortune 50 companies such as Microsoft, AT&T, United Health Group, Fannie Mae, and State Farm.

Prior to becoming a speaker, he was a leadership professor and stand-up comedian. He also managed nonprofit enterprises that provided employment for people with disabilities.

In between presentations, David competes in ultramarathons and Ironman triathlons.

David has a doctor of management degree in organizational leadership, as well as a graduate degree in psychology. He is the author of four books:

1. The Four Factors of Effective Leadership

2. The Freak Factor

3. The Freak Factor for Kids

4. Pink Goldfish

Contact David at drendall.com

About the illustrator

Eric Smoldt grew up in Iowa, went to college in Illinois, and now lives in Indiana with his wife and three children.

He is a graphic artist and photographer. He has worked in the visual arts field for 25 years, the last 14 at a Big 10 university.

See more of Eric's work at ericsmoldt.com

Made in the USA
Columbia, SC
21 February 2022

56564817R00029